THE
LIFE
OF
ST.
PAUL

THE LIFE OF ST. PAUL

TEXT BY
Lawrence Boadt, CSP

PAINTINGS BY
LINDA SCHAPPER

Paulist Press
New York/Mahwah, NJ

Scripture quotations are taken from the author's own translation. The Scripture quote on p. 3 is taken from the New American Bible. Revised New Testament of the New American Bible copyright © 1986 by the Confraternity of Christian Doctrine.

Caseside design by Sharyn Banks
Interior design by Lynn Else

Library of Congress Cataloging-in-Publication Data

Boadt, Lawrence.
    The life of St. Paul / text by Lawrence Boadt ; paintings by Linda Schapper.
        p. cm.
    Includes bibliographical references.
    ISBN-13: 978-0-8091-0519-9 (alk. paper)
    1. Paul, the Apostle, Saint. 2. Apostles—Biography. I. Title.
    BS2506.3.B63 2008
    225.9′2—dc22

                                                              2008014545

Published by Paulist Press
997 Macarthur Boulevard
Mahwah, New Jersey 07430

www.paulistpress.com

Printed and bound in Mexico

CONTENTS

ILLUSTRATIONS

WHY SHOULD WE KNOW ST. PAUL?

Most people probably think first of the four Gospels when asked, "What is the most important part of the New Testament?" In the sense that we must have the story of Jesus before we can reflect on it, they are right. The Gospels must come first. But it can be easily argued that Paul is more important to the whole structure of the New Testament and how we understand it than any of the Gospel writers individually would be. First of all, he is the earliest Christian voice in the history of the church. His letters were all composed between 48 and 64 AD, and almost all scholars date the earliest Gospel, Mark, to a few years later, during or after the Great Jewish Revolt against Rome, from 66 to 70 AD. So, in Paul's Letters we are able to look into the very heart of the first apostolic preaching of the Good News of Jesus and its major points of emphasis even before there was a written account in a formal Gospel. Second, through the decision of Luke some years later to continue his own Gospel with the story of Peter and Paul in the Acts of the Apostles, we are able to read the first biography of a Christian believer. His arrangement of Paul's life into missionary journeys gives us a very human portrait of a man of vision and great energy, who often endured much suffering and bore it willingly for the sake of his mission and, at the same time, a man filled with great confidence and trust in the power of God's grace in his life. Third, Paul's theological insight and manner of expressing the meaning of Jesus' death and resurrection was not only the first work of Christian theology, but still stands unequaled above all subsequent efforts. His theology of God's plan of salvation unveiled in the life, death, and resurrection of Jesus that brought about "the forgiveness of sins…the resurrection of the dead, and the life of the world to come" (as the Nicene Creed puts it) is also a profound spirituality of union with the risen Christ through the power of the Holy Spirit that gives full praise and glory to the Father. Finally,

Paul is a model for all Christians to imitate. He recognized the importance of the risen Jesus intervening in his life at his conversion and then guiding his growth and life of dedication in all the years after. He frequently cited to new converts the need to imitate himself.

For all these reasons it is a privilege to tell the story of Paul once again, and to invite the readers to discover his faith and knowledge of Christ, as well as his astounding personality, while also meditating on the unique iconlike paintings of Linda Schapper. She captures the essence of each scene and its edge of mystery with the simplest of visual settings, merely suggesting the drama of a moment without trying to describe it so realistically that nothing is left for our imagination. Indeed, she forces us to imagine Paul's experience, and forces us back to the power of the New Testament texts to discover Paul for ourselves.

Chapter 1

WHO IS THIS PAUL, THE APOSTLE?

We know more about Paul than about any other person in the New Testament because he wrote perhaps thirteen of its twenty-seven books and revealed a lot about himself in the course of his letters. But even more, he is the hero of St. Luke's second volume, the Acts of the Apostles, and Luke draws a very detailed portrait of Paul as a missionary. Even with all of this, however, Paul remains somewhat of a mystery to later ages. We have little information about life for a Jew in the remote town of Tarsus in southern Turkey where he was born; and we are not sure exactly how this young boy, first trained as a tentmaker, became a rabbinic student of Gamaliel, one of the leading teachers in Jerusalem itself. We also wonder how this fierce persecutor of the Christians could suddenly become their most passionate preacher. We know almost nothing about what he did as a new Christian for nearly ten to twelve years before he suddenly became active in Antioch in Syria. And finally, there is no certainty concerning the facts of his death, except that everyone agrees it probably took place in Rome during Nero's reign—but was it in 64 or 68 AD?

We may not be able to solve all the details of his life, but we can certainly draw a profile of his work and thought as a missionary between 47 or 48 and 60 AD. We can then add many small pieces from the early period of his life mentioned in the Acts of the Apostles or from the later traditions about his death as best we can.

Paul enters the biblical story at the stoning of the deacon Stephen in Acts 7:58, where it tells us that the enraged crowd piled their cloaks at the feet of "a young man named Saul" while they cast their rocks at the church's first martyr. If we assume he was between eighteen and twenty years old, he would have been born between 14 and 16 AD. But what if he were twenty-five or more, having studied long years under Gamaliel? Then he would have been born closer to 8 to 10 AD. St. Luke in his Acts of the Apostles tells us in 22:3 that Paul was born in Tarsus of Cilicia but was brought up in Jerusalem. The only fact we know about his education is from the same passage, where Paul says he was taught a strict interpretation of the Jewish Law under Gamaliel. Luke continually calls him by his original Jewish name, Saul, until he devotes himself primarily to working with the pagans—from then on he is known to all by the Roman equivalent name, Paul.

Chapter 2

TARSUS OF CILICIA, "NO MEAN CITY" (ACTS 21:39)

In Acts 21:39, Paul tells the Roman commander in Jerusalem that he is a citizen of the city of Tarsus, and in 25:11 he appeals for direct trial before the emperor because he also has full rights as a Roman citizen. Today, Tarsus is a rather small and pleasant town with very few signs of Roman remains—the most prominent being a triumphal arch commemorating the visit of the emperor Hadrian, which was erected seventy years after Paul's death. Nothing certain from the time of Paul can be seen at all, and most of the Roman ruins are still twenty feet under the modern streets not yet excavated by archaeologists. If they were brought to light they would reveal that in the first century Tarsus was no backwater. It was a flourishing Roman colony with a long previous history. Its very name means "hoof" and stems from the Greek myth that the famed winged horse Pegasus lost one of its hooves in Tarsus. The city was strategically located ten miles up the Cnidus River from the sea and thirty miles below the narrow pass of the "Cilician Gates" through which all traffic from Anatolia and Cappadocia in central Turkey would travel to the Near East. Some tests have shown there are signs of a city dating back to 2500 BC on the site. And it was well known in second-millennium BC Hittite documents such as "Tarsa in Kizzuwatna" (Cilicia). It came under the control of the Assyrians in the ninth century BC and is mentioned by name in the famed "Black Obelisk" of King Shalmaneser III from 841, which is now on display in the British Museum. Xenophon reported in the fifth century BC that Tarsus was a large and prosperous city, and Alexander the Great stopped there in his campaign to conquer the

3

Persians and nearly died of fever after swimming in the cold waters of the Cydnus River that goes past the town.

In 67 BC Pompey added it to the Roman Empire. It welcomed Cicero as its proconsul for the year 51–50 BC and was wildly supportive of Julius Caesar when he visited. Following the assassination of Julius Caesar, it sided with Mark Antony against Brutus and Cassius, and was rewarded by being named a free Roman city. It was also the scene of the famous meeting of Mark Antony and Cleopatra in 41 BC. Antony had just defeated Cassius at the Battle of Philippi, and the young queen of Egypt, who had supported Cassius, realized she had better make peace with the victor. She sailed to meet him at Tarsus, and through her wiles and beauty she succeeded in seducing the Roman general. They became lovers for a decade before being defeated by Octavius, the future emperor Augustus.

In Paul's time, some years later, the people of Tarsus were famous for their intellectual curiosity, and the Roman geographer Strabo reported that they had more schools for philosophy than Athens itself! It also had numerous schools of rhetoric. We can easily understand where Paul got his skill in speaking and interest in philosophy that Luke so frequently notes. Unfortunately, a century later, Philostratus reports that the people of Tarsus had lost their interest in learning and were addicted to lazy luxury and indulgence. Paul himself did not stay long in Tarsus to study but was sent at a young age to get a full rabbinic education in Jerusalem under Gamaliel (Acts 22:3). This may be reflected in Paul's very sketchy use of Greek philosophy in his writings. But he was very proud of being a Roman citizen when he appealed to the emperor for justice in Acts 25:11. That an ordinary person, and a Jew besides, could hold Roman citizenship was very rare. Tarsus was first granted the privilege of full citizenship in the Seleucid kingdom by King Antiochus Epiphanes (175–164 BC) as a reward for its support against his enemies. When the Romans took over, they continued to respect the special status of the city and confirmed the privilege of Roman citizenship.

Chapter 3

STEPHEN BEFORE THE SANHEDRIN

Before St. Luke introduces us to St. Paul in his Acts of the Apostles, he prepares for Paul's ministry by telling the story of the first martyr of the early church, the deacon Stephen, in Acts 6 and 7. Although Acts 6:2 suggests that Stephen was among those deacons chosen to take care of the physical needs of the disciples while the apostles preached and prayed, all the following descriptions assume that these deacons also preached the Gospel and healed those who came to them for help. Among them, Stephen proved to be the most eloquent, so much so that the Jewish leaders plotted to arrest him on charges that he blasphemed Moses and God by stating that the Temple could be destroyed and the laws of sacrifice ended.

He was tried before the Sanhedrin. It was composed of leading citizens and priests of Jerusalem, who had the responsibility to preserve public order among the people, oversee judicial cases, regulate religious teachings, and represent the people's concerns to the Roman administration. The term *Sanhedrin* was a term used for any assembly called by leaders for special purposes. In particular some served as a kind of ongoing advisory legislature for the governor or other leaders. The Jerusalem Sanhedrin may have been the primary advisory body to the high priest. It may also have judged questions of violations of the Law, particularly capital cases, but this is not clearly stated in any historical accounts. The Gospels tell us that, when called to put Jesus on trial by the high priest, the Jerusalem Sanhedrin needed to ask the Romans for permission before it could carry out its death sentence. But in the case of Stephen, it apparently acted immediately to put Stephen to death.

Luke presents the defense of Stephen before the Sanhedrin as an eloquent retelling of the entire salvation history in the Old Testament. But in it

7

he highlights how each generation out of jealousy rejected the very leader whom God had sent to them, even Moses, their first teacher of the Law. Moreover he emphasized that although God had promised to dwell with Israel, he had never insisted on the permanence of the Temple or of the sacrifices required by the Law. Instead he had sent the prophets to warn them to turn back to him, but the people had rejected the words of the prophets, finally even rejecting Jesus, the Just One, who was the last and greatest prophet whom God had sent. For the Sanhedrin this was proof enough that the charges were true and that Stephen deserved death by stoning.

Chapter 4

THE STONING OF STEPHEN

While Stephen was testifying before the Sanhedrin, Saul, as a student of Gamaliel, one of its leading figures, presumably would have been waiting near the doors until his master came out. Having been carefully taught the prevailing interpretations of the Law, young Saul would have agreed fully with their anger and the decision to condemn Stephen. Thus he would have heard the uproar of the members of the assembly as they shouted Stephen down and condemned him to death. No doubt this was a very exciting day for the young apprentice rabbi, and he probably joined in the shouting against this traitor. He was doubly pleased that the senior leaders asked him to watch their cloaks and robes while they found stones to cast at Stephen (Acts 7:58). As Saul observed his elders become aroused to fever pitch and then as a group begin to stone Stephen, Luke tells us that he approved of the killing (Acts 8:1).

Stoning was the ordinary means of execution all through Israel's history. Stones are the most common material available in the deserts and hills of Palestine for use in killing. If done as a formal sentence of death, the entire community must take part in the stoning after removing the offender outside the city or camp. Then the two witnesses who had accused the person were to lay their hands on the criminal's head and cast the first stone themselves (Lev 24:14–16; Num 15:36; Deut 17:5–7). The main crimes for which stoning was prescribed were idolatry, adultery, sorcery, breaking the Sabbath, and disrespect for parents. Blasphemy or violating holy things would be generally included (see Exod 19:13; Lev 24:14; Josh 7:25; John 10:31–33).

The Sanhedrin then launched a persecution against the small Christian community throughout Jerusalem that probably extended outward to all of Judea, Samaria, and Galilee, since the apostles and deacons were dispersed all

9

over the area (Acts 8:4). Saul, certainly feeling a part of a great effort to stamp out these heretical followers of Jesus, joined in wholeheartedly, dragging people from their homes and throwing them in jail. His zeal grew so great that he even asked the high priest for letters authorizing him to arrest any Christians found in far-off Damascus and bring them back to Jerusalem for trial (Acts 9:1). Later, in Acts 22:20, Paul will explain his role in these words: "While the blood of your witness Stephen was being shed, I stood by and approved it. I even guarded the cloaks of those who slew him!" Little did Paul realize that his life was about to change for good!

Chapter 5

PAUL'S CONVERSION

The most important event in Paul's life was his conversion on the road to Damascus. St. Luke emphasizes this by reporting the event three separate times in his Acts of the Apostles. In the first, Acts 9:1–19, Luke narrates it as a story; in the second, Acts 22:1–21, Paul himself tells the Jews in Jerusalem his story; and in the third, Acts 26:9–23, Paul tells the story to King Agrippa, who was ruler over part of Northern Galilee. Each account agrees on the fundamental facts, but each has its own additions and variations. The basic outline of events tells how Paul was on his way to Damascus to arrest Christians; just outside the city he was struck down by an overwhelming light and heard a voice; when he got up he was blind and had to be led to Damascus to a house where he stayed without relief. Meanwhile, his companions were also struck by the light and heard the sound of the voice but saw no one. God then stirred Ananias, one of the leading Christians of Damascus, to go to Paul and announce that God intended to send Paul as missionary to the pagan peoples. After Ananias had placed his hands on Paul and announced God's message to him, Saul was healed and immediately received baptism.

The first account accents the role of Ananias in bringing God's commission to Paul, but the third account never even mentions Ananias. In the second and third accounts Paul recounts his extensive role as persecutor in some detail, while it is barely mentioned in the first account. In all three versions, the voice announces that it is Jesus of Nazareth whom Paul was persecuting, but in the third account, Jesus adds the sentence, "It is hard to kick against the goad!" (Acts 26:14). This phrase means that Paul would not find it easy to refuse God's commission. Both the first and second accounts highlight that Paul is being set aside to bring the Gospel to the Gentile pagans rather than the Jews, but in the third account, before the Jewish king, Paul chooses to highlight that he preached just as much to the Jews as to the pagans. All in all, Luke gives great attention to this single moment of Paul's conversion as the turning point of the Gospel. Up until then, the apostles had mainly preached the Gospel only to Jews, but from this moment on, the church will no longer be primarily Jewish but will become a universal church for all peoples. While the Jewish Christians will remain small, and even eventually disappear by the fifth century, the Gentile church will grow and spread across the world.

Chapter 6

PAUL'S BAPTISM

According to the first account of Paul's conversion in Acts 9:17–19, Ananias went to the house where Paul was staying after being blinded and, while laying hands on him, told Paul that the Lord Jesus had both sent him to restore Paul's sight and allow him to receive the Holy Spirit. The text goes on, however, to say that "immediately something like scales fell from Saul's eyes and his sight was restored," but he did not begin to act like a man filled with the Spirit. Instead he got up and was baptized and then took something to eat to regain his strength. Only a few days later did he begin, as a man filled with the Holy Spirit, to preach zealously about Jesus to all who would listen (Acts 9:20–21). The second version of his conversion in Acts 22:12–16 gives a slightly fuller account of Ananias's words. He adds a further commission from the Lord: "The God of our ancestors has chosen you to know his will, to see the Righteous One, and to hear his own voice; for you will be his witness to all the world of what you have seen and heard. And now why do you delay? Get up, be baptized, and have your sins washed away, calling on his name!"

Thus Paul was to enter the church the same way that every convert after the ascension of the Lord joins the community of believers, through baptism. He was not like the original twelve apostles, even Matthias who entered late (Acts 1:21–26), who did not need baptism because they had known Jesus while he was on earth. Thus from the beginning all new members who have heard about Jesus from the church must enter it by baptism. Peter insisted on it for the very first converts on Pentecost Day itself in Acts 2:38. Paul was no different, even though he received a special apostolic commission from Jesus himself. Not having known the earthly Jesus, he received faith in the risen Lord as God's gift, but came to know him through the union with Christ created

15

by baptism. As Paul tells us so pointedly in Romans 6:3–4: "Do you not know that all of us who have been baptized into Christ Jesus were baptized into his death...so that, just as Christ was raised from the dead by the glory of the Father, so we too might walk in newness of life." He goes on to say that we will share in both the risen life of Jesus and in his forgiveness of sins through his death (Rom 6:5–6).

Chapter 7

PAUL'S FIRST YEARS AS A CHRISTIAN

Paul recounts his first actions as a Christian with great passion in his Letter to the Galatians, chapter 2. There he tells us that after receiving the command to bring the Gospel to the Gentiles from Ananias, he did not immediately do so, but spent time alone in Arabia without consulting any of the Christian apostles and leaders (Gal 1:16–17). At some point he returned to Damascus and spent three years there among the Christians and preaching to the Jews. Some of them conspired to kill him and watched for an opportunity to capture him, but the disciples lowered him secretly by night over the walls of Damascus in a basket (Acts 9:25). He then went up to Jerusalem to meet Peter. He spent fifteen days with Peter and did meet also with James, the brother of the Lord. He also preached the Gospel boldly as he had in Damascus until once again the Jews tried to kill him. The apostles sent him away from Jerusalem and in Caesarea put him on a ship for Syria and then on to his hometown of Tarsus in Cilicia. We do not know whether he preached there or stayed in solitude. Meanwhile the church grew strongly in Antioch, the capital of Syria, and many Gentiles asked to be baptized. This forced the church to ask the Jerusalem leaders for guidance on the question of admitting pagans who were not Jews, and they sent Barnabas to check on the situation. He saw immediately that it was the work of God's Spirit, and so he sought out Saul in Tarsus and brought him to Antioch to assist in the work of conversion among these Gentile seekers.

Antioch was located five miles above the mouth of the Orontes River, with its main port of Seleucia on the seacoast itself. It was founded in 300 BC by Seleucus, one of the generals who succeeded Alexander the Great. It sat on the edge of a very fertile plain, and the passes through the surrounding mountains funneled trade from the north and the east to its port. When the Romans captured it in 64 BC, it became a major base for their military control of the eastern empire. It grew greatly over the years until it was the third largest city in the Roman Empire. Population estimates range from 200,000 to 600,000 people in the third century AD, but in the time of Paul, the population was probably closer to 100,000. Jews had been among the earliest settlers of Antioch, and their community was quite large, but their situation had always been difficult, since several riots and attacks against the Jewish population are recorded from Roman times. According to Acts 11, it seems that, early on, many Jews as well as Gentiles had become Christians there. Scholars have often suggested that both Matthew's and Luke's Gospels were written in Antioch, and Galatians 2 places Peter there as well. It was indeed a good base for the Christian missionaries.

Chapter 8

PAUL'S FIRST MISSIONARY JOURNEY

Acts 13 opens with the Holy Spirit inspiring the church at Antioch to send out Saul and Barnabas for missionary work in Turkey. At that time, modern Turkey was the heart of the Greek-speaking world, and its great cities of Antioch and Ephesus were the leading centers of Hellenistic-Roman culture. It was densely populated with many medium-size towns and cities, all with their Greek theaters, gymnasiums, and monuments of Roman and Greek culture, and most had sizable Jewish communities like the one in Tarsus from which Paul had come. This was fertile ground for an eloquent homegrown preacher that knew his audience well!

Saul and Barnabas undertook their first missionary trip, planning to go to the center of the southern area of Turkey. But first they sailed from Antioch to Cyprus and spent some time preaching throughout the island. Cyprus is 138 miles long by 68 miles wide, and traces of early settlements go back to 7000 BC. It had been known to the ancient Hittites and Egyptians as Alishia, and as Elishah in Genesis 10:4 and Ezekiel 27:7. It was also identified as Kittim in Genesis 10:4 and elsewhere after its major city, the Phoenician port of Kition, which is modern Larnaka. It was the chief source of copper for the ancient world. In the *Iliad* and *Odyssey*, Homer even calls the island *kupros*, the word for copper, from which it gets its modern name. When the Sea Peoples destroyed the great kingdom of the Minoans on Crete in 1380 BC, many of its refugees fled to Cyprus and introduced strong Mycenaean influences to its art and pottery. Cypriote pottery was highly valued, and exported examples are found in every country around the Mediterranean. Later, the Phoenicians established settlements on the eastern end, and through their extensive shipping network extended the trade from Cyprus even farther west. The island had supported

Alexander the Great in capturing the Phoenician capital of Tyre, and was ruled by the Egyptian branch of the Greek rulers, the Ptolemies, from 321 down to the Roman conquest of 57 BC. Cyprus was then joined with Cilicia as part of the Roman Province of Syria, whose capital was Antioch. But in 27 BC, Augustus made it a separate province of its own and gave it to the senate to appoint a proconsul. Luke rightly notes this in Acts 13:7 when naming Sergius Paulus as the proconsul.

The missionaries would have found extensive Roman roads and well-developed cities mostly on the eastern end of the island. The people lived mostly by agriculture, copper production, and commercial shipping from its many port cities. Barnabas, the apostle who had called Paul to this mission, was a native of Cyprus. The two apostles began their missionary work in Salamis, which had a large enough Jewish population to have more than one synagogue, but then moved across the island to Paphos, the provincial capital, to meet with the proconsul. It is there that Acts first calls the apostle by his Roman name, Paul. He was now clearly working primarily in the Gentile world. It is also in Paphos that he rebuked the magician Bar-Jesus as a false prophet and had God strike the man blind temporarily. This greatly impresses Sergius Paulus, but there is no indication he was baptized at that time. Some inscriptions a century or more later, however, do suggest that later members of his family were among the Christians.

After their stay in Cyprus they sailed on to Perga, a coastal town of Pamphylia in modern Turkey, and went inland to the cities of Antioch of Pisidia, Iconium, Lystra, and Derbe. In each town they preached first to the Jews and then to the pagan Gentiles, and won many converts in each place, but also met resistance from dedicated zealots of the Law who succeeded in making them move on when they began to have great success. Finally, they went back by the same way that they had come, and after reaching Perga, had to go on to Attalia to catch a ship back to Antioch. They carefully appointed presbyters, that is, elders, in each town to govern the community after they had left. This first journey probably lasted less than a year but had shown the great hunger for the Gospel among the Gentiles.

Luke pauses in recounting the details of this journey to give us a detailed account of Paul's technique as he taught in Antioch of Pisidia in Acts 13:13–52. Paul spoke first to the Jews in the synagogue on the Sabbath and, using the Old Testament history of salvation, discussed the prophecies of the coming Messiah, how Jesus fulfilled the prophetic hopes, and how God verified it by raising him from the dead. Many believed this great promise of ever-lasting life, but others found it blasphemous and prevented Paul from returning. So he spoke on the next Sabbath in a public place and won over many Gentiles. His success with reaching the Gentiles was so great that Paul and Barnabas focused specially on the pagans from that moment forward. The meaning of Jesus' words that he was to be an instrument to bring Jesus' name to the Gentiles (Acts 9:15) and to be a witness to the whole world (Acts 22:15) were becoming clearer. Paul nevertheless made it a policy to always preach first in the local synagogue because he would always find at least some who welcomed his message among the "God-Fearers," devout pagans who attended Jewish services but could not bring themselves to undergo circumcision and follow kosher food rules. When rejected by a synagogue community, many of these God-Fearers followed Paul to a new location and became converts.

Chapter 9

PAUL, STONED AND LEFT FOR DEAD

Pisidian Antioch was not technically in Pisidia at all, but in the territory of Phrygia that had been included in the new province of Galatia in 25 BC. It was some 3600 feet high on the inland plateau. It had been awarded status as a Roman colony by Augustus, and so was a good place for Paul's preaching. He favored the cities that had special status in the Roman Empire, such as Philippi or Thessalonica or here, because they were situated on the strategic highways that linked the Empire. Paul enjoyed much initial success in this Antioch, but the town leaders soon forced Paul and Barnabas to leave, and they made their way to Iconium. They won many over in the synagogue in this town also, but once again Jewish leaders stirred up the congregation to drive Paul out. He and Barnabas then moved on to the province of Lycaonia and its city of Lystra. Here, the local people at first tried to worship the apostles as gods because Paul cured a crippled man so he could walk. But once again, they were forced to leave Lystra when some Jews came from Pisidian Antioch and turned the Jewish community against him. They even attempted to stone him to death (Acts 14:19), but he survived, and his supporters helped him to move on to Derbe.

Paul was being constantly forced to move on because of the determination of the established Jewish communities not to allow the message of Jesus to be preached in their synagogues, or even to allow Paul to stay in their area. Groups had forced him to leave Antioch in Pisidia when both Jews and Gentiles had accepted his message so readily, and again in Iconium and Lystra. These experiences brought home to Paul the words the risen Lord had spoken to Ananias when he was sent to Paul, "I myself will show him how much he must

suffer for the sake of my name" (Acts 9:16). Paul would always concentrate on the "Good News" of salvation in the resurrection of Jesus, but only when his hearers first believed wholeheartedly in the suffering and death of Jesus given for the forgiveness of their sins. The message of the cross was at the heart of Paul's preaching. He would say eloquently in 1 Corinthians 1:17, "For Christ did not send me to baptize but to proclaim the Gospel...so that the cross of Christ might not be emptied of its power." A few sentences later, he adds, "...we proclaim Christ crucified—a stumbling block to Jews and foolishness to Gentiles" (1 Cor 1:23).

Suffering was to be part of Paul's ministry from the beginning. He does not speak often of the physical attacks he endured, but does give one impassioned listing in his Second Letter to the Corinthians. Only in Lystra was he stoned, but he was beaten three times, shipwrecked three times, and always in danger from those who pursued him (2 Cor 11:23–27). But his real suffering came from his concern for his churches and their faith. He constantly anguished over their ability to persist in following the teachings of Jesus and their love for one another. He can correct and complain loudly and often in his letters, hoping to bring people to their senses. Strong passages of such concern can be found in 1 and 2 Corinthians, Galatians, 1 and 2 Thessalonians, and in his Letter to Philemon.

Chapter 10

THE COUNCIL
OF JERUSALEM

The success of Paul and Barnabas in winning over the pagans to Christ on such a large scale led to the first great crisis for the still small Christian community. Were they a part of Judaism whose only major difference was that they believed in Jesus as the Messiah rather than in someone else? Or were they now a new and changed faith that welcomed Gentiles as well as Jews into a new covenant relationship that was centered on Christ rather than the Law and Temple? This was particularly troublesome to the church of Jerusalem where all the members were observant Jews as well as followers of Christ, and who held strongly that they must each live as Jesus had done, as a faithful Jew, in order to be his follower. Since Roman and Greek men found circumcision to be a mark of shame, it was hard for them to accept this requirement. Paul, and according to Luke in Acts 9–11, also Peter, had come to the conclusion that the Holy Spirit was being given to Gentile individuals and even whole families before they followed any Jewish observance, and so God was clearly marking the Gentiles for salvation apart from any observance of the Law. This was exactly Peter's experience of converting the Roman centurion Cornelius in Acts 10—11, and it matched what Paul and Barnabas had found in their mission to Turkey.

Paul and Barnabas went back to Jerusalem to argue the case before the apostles, and both Acts 15 and Galatians 2 describe the great debate with major speeches by Peter and James, but in the end, the apostles realized that the Holy Spirit indeed was pointing a different way for the Gentiles. The only restrictions they set were that Gentiles must respect the sensitivities to the most sacred things in Jewish practice for the sake of harmony and common discipleship: (1) not eating food offered to false statues of the gods in Roman temples as though it were ordinary food; (2) not eating blood in their meat, which would violate kosher laws; and (3) not marrying close relatives as specified by Jewish Law, in order to avoid the lax and often scandalous marriages between siblings or in-laws that pagans tolerated.

Chapter 11

THE SECOND MISSIONARY JOURNEY: PHILIPPI

Paul was soon called to make a second journey through the places where he had already gone. This time Barnabas went his own way, but Paul retraced his steps through central Turkey and on to the northwestern coast. Along the way, needing help, Paul returned to Lystra to convince an enthusiastic young man, Timothy, to join him in his work. When they reached the coast of the Aegean Sea, Paul experienced a dream in which he saw a "man from Macedonia" calling him to come to preach to the Macedonians. As a result, he and Timothy set sail from Troy to reach the town of Neapolis along the northern coast of Greece. Although it had become part of the territory of Macedonia under Philip II of Macedon and his son Alexander the Great, Neapolis was technically located in ancient Thrace, whose people were known as warriors and considered to be so wild as to be nearly barbarians. This was the port for the most important city of the area, Philippi, which stood ten miles to the northwest of Neapolis. The city had been founded in 360 BC by Greek settlers from the island of Thasos under the exiled Athenian leader Kallistratos. But Philip II quickly annexed it to his empire to protect the precious metal mines found on Mount Pangaion that overlooked the city. The Romans took control of the city in the second century BC and made Philippi an outpost on its major road to the east, the *Via Egnatia*. Its most important moment came when Mark Antony and Octavian defeated Brutus and Cassius, the assassins of Julius Caesar, at the battle of Philippi in 42 BC. In gratitude for the victory, they named the city a free Roman colony and settled many veterans there in the next few years. After Octavian later defeated Antony at the Battle of Actium in 30 BC, more veterans

were brought in and given land. Thus, while the people of the city were mostly Roman colonists, there were still many Thracian natives as well in the city, and both groups responded positively to Paul's preaching. It became his favorite city, as we learn later from his famous Letter to the Philippians, in which he constantly thanks them for their generosity and support of his work.

It was at Philippi that Paul met Lydia, who was a quite successful businesswoman in this coastal city of Macedonia. Acts 16 says she was from Thyatira, a city some miles from Ephesus on the Turkish coast. Obviously she had moved from there to this trading center, which saw merchants and ships from all parts of the Roman Empire. Purple dye came from murex shells, most prominently found along the Lebanese coast, but also from other coastal waters. It was so scarce and hard to produce that it was reserved for dying the togas and special robes of high officials and royal persons. Acts 16:14 also tells us that she was a "God-fearer," that is, one who was a Gentile but admired and prayed with the Jewish people, without being willing to officially become a Jew. She was struck by Paul's preaching and asked that both she and her household be baptized by Paul. Because she was a successful merchant, she probably had a large home, and she prevailed on Paul and his party to stay at her house while in Philippi. They did so for their entire time in the city, even returning to say good-bye when forced to leave the area by the authorities in Acts 16:40.

Despite common claims that Paul did not like women, this story of Lydia and the passages about his deep friendship with Pricilla and Aquila (Acts 18:1–2, 18; Rom 16:3; 1 Cor 16:19) and his mention of many other female co-workers, deaconesses, and generous women in the concluding paragraphs of his letters to the Romans and Corinthians reveal a Paul who appreciated the women in his life, worked closely with them, and valued their friendship.

Chapter 12

PAUL IMPRISONED AT PHILIPPI

Despite the warm reception Paul received from many like Lydia at Philippi, it was also the place where Paul ended up in prison because of a new problem—namely, the fear of pagans that Christianity threatened their way of life. Thus Acts 16 tells how he freed a magician's assistant from her possession by an evil spirit, and the angry owner, who had now lost his major source of income, denounced Paul before the Roman courts as destructive of Roman ways. Philippi was well known for its numerous pagan shrines and temples to Hercules, Bacchus, Dionysius, and Artemis throughout the city and a famous shrine of the oracle of Dionysius nearby on Mount Pangaion. These cults, which stressed ecstatic behavior, were clearly typical of the area. Inscriptions at these shrines also reveal a great predominance of women devotees, and so both the scene of Paul curing the possessed girl and the importance of Lydia as a religious leader are all very much at home in the culture of Philippi.

That same night, as Paul and his companions were chained in prison, an earthquake toppled the jail and broke the walls and their chains. The jailer was about to kill himself, thinking he had lost his prisoners, when Paul reassured him they had not run off. As a result the jailer and his family were converted and baptized by Paul. This is the second time in the same stay that Paul had baptized an entire family. Although infant baptism was not the normal practice for the sacrament in New Testament stories, it is certainly indicated in these stories of Lydia and the jailer. In general, most people came to believe in Jesus as adults because they had heard the apostles preach the Good News. They would then ask to be baptized. In contrast, we have little in the way of evidence outside of these two stories in Acts that children also would be baptized when their parents converted. But it can be assumed that, despite the fact that almost all our evidence is for adult baptism, children were often included when whole families became Christian. For example, there is no evidence that they were excluded or had to be baptized separately when they reached a certain age. This no doubt followed the many injunctions of Jesus himself to let the little children come to him (see Matt 18:1–5; 19:13–15). The sacrament of baptism was thus not understood mostly as a necessary confirmation of one's personal act of belief in Jesus, but rather as an incorporation into the body of Christ, in which, as a community, all shared in its power to forgive sin and to bring eternal life and the possession of the Holy Spirit.

The ruins of Philippi are still impressive today. They contain a fine Roman forum and two magnificent Roman basilicas as well as several other important buildings. But most of them were built after the time of Paul during Philippi's golden age in the second century AD under the emperors Hadrian and Antoninus Pius. In the period after Constantine officially recognized Christianity in the fourth century, Christian churches and shrines multiplied so that Philippi was known as a city of churches. Unfortunately, the one building shown to all tourists as authentically Pauline, the so-called "prison" in which Paul was kept, has very little authenticity to support its claims.

Acts 16 concludes Paul's stay in Philippi and his release from prison by noting that the Spirit continued to watch over him and grant him success in proclaiming the Gospel of Jesus.

Chapter 13

PAUL ARRIVES AT THESSALONICA

Thessalonica was the major city in the north of Greece, some sixty miles west of Philippi. It had been founded in 319 BC by Cassander, whom Alexander the Great had placed in charge of his Macedonian kingdom when he moved his army east to defeat the Persians. He named the city after Thessalonike, Alexander's sister and last surviving member of the royal family. It was strategically placed at the head of the Thermaikos Gulf and had a wonderful circular beachfront ringed by high hills providing natural protection. The Romans conquered the area in 168 BC and divided Macedonia into four provinces, making Thessalonica the capital of one. When the local people rose in revolt in 146, the Romans deported the entire Macedonian upper class to Italy. Because Thessalonica was on the Egnatian Way, it enjoyed the benefits of extensive commercial traffic. During the Roman civil wars of the first century BC, it sided first with Pompey in 48 BC, then with Brutus and Cassius in 44 BC, and then switched sides to Mark Antony at the Battle of Philippi in 42, and even named the period as the "Era of Antony." When finally Octavian emerged as the single victor and emperor after the Battle of Actium in 30 BC, Thessalonica switched sides again. The city built temples and grand statues in honor of Augustus, as the emperor was now called. This enthusiastic and very politically astute glorification of the emperor and his *pax romana* (world peace) may have inspired Paul to condemn those who seek "peace and security" above God in his letter to the city (1 Thess 5:3).

Thessalonica was also the home to a Jewish synagogue. Acts 17:1–4 tells us that Paul spent three weeks in a row at the Sabbath services presenting his case for Jesus as the Messiah promised to the Jewish people, and arguing the case that God did not desire his Messiah to be a victorious military conqueror

in the model of a royal David, but to be a lowly servant, intending for Jesus to undergo suffering and be crucified in order to save Israel. Some of the Jewish men converted, but Paul had more success with women and the God-fearing Gentiles who attended the synagogue services on the side. Once again this led the Jews who opposed what he was saying to stir up anger against Paul and accuse him as a disruptive troublemaker and seek to drive him out of the city. They even formed a gang who attacked the synagogue leader Jason's house and dragged him before the city magistrate for permitting Paul to speak in the synagogue. But the Roman officials allowed Jason to post bail and then released him and his family—putting the whole incident down, no doubt, to the constant bickering typical of zealous religious groups.

The next day, the believing disciples sent Paul away to the next large town of Beroea where, Luke tells us, Paul was received more warmly than he had been in Thessalonica. Yet those Thessalonians who had believed in Paul's teaching and become Christians must have been extremely dedicated to the Gospel and very faithful to Paul in light of the persecution they underwent. As a result, he directed his earliest letter that we know of to the Christians at Thessalonica, what we call First Thessalonians. In it, unlike any other letter that he later wrote, he dedicates the first three chapters as a whole to expressing his confidence in their faith and gratitude for their steadfast loyalty to what he had taught them despite the fierce persecution they had endured to do so. He especially emphasizes that he had always been gentle with them and never made demands on them for support, while urging them to continue to give witness to other local towns and communities. Paul goes on in 1 Thessalonians 3:1–10 to identify closely with this community in their suffering for the Gospel, noting that he had told them of his suffering when he was with them, and now from what had been reported back to him about their distress, felt they were one in this together.

Extensive Roman ruins have been found throughout the modern city, but none that can be directly connected to the visit of Paul reported in Acts 17.

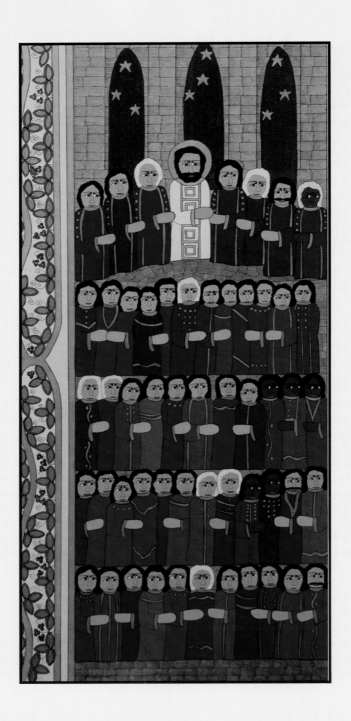

Chapter 14

PAUL'S BRIEF STAY IN ATHENS

Paul enjoyed great success in Beroea as he had in Philippi, winning over many leading women members of the Jewish community and many Gentiles. But the same Jewish opponents followed him all the way from Thessalonica to drive him out of Beroea, and soon he was on the road south to Athens. It was in Athens that Paul met his first great setback in preaching the Gospel. Athens was the home of many of the leading schools of philosophy in Greece, and the citizens prided themselves on a reputation as great thinkers. Apparently from what Luke says in Acts 17:19–21, many Athenians had the leisure to frequent the public places of debate daily. Paul preached on the Sabbath to the members of the Jewish synagogue, as he did everywhere he went, but on the other days of the week he sought out the public squares to argue that he had a new faith better than the ones they constantly debated about. The Athenians were uncertain whether this was just some Asian religious sect similar to the many others that had passed through the city, or whether it was truly a new school of philosophy. A group made up mostly of Stoics and Epicureans invited Paul to present the case for his beliefs at the Areopagus, the center for philosophical discussion. Paul leaped at the chance to preach the Gospel, using as his starting point that Athens was full of cults of different gods, including even a statue to the "Unknown God." Paul then declared that what had been to them an unknown God was now revealed in the message of Jesus of Nazareth. He argued carefully, in his best philosophical language, that God indeed made the universe and all peoples, Jews and pagans alike, but remained unknown as people searched in the wrong ways for him. Now he had appointed his Son to call the world back to himself, but did so by permitting his death in order to establish his resurrection as the source of everlasting life.

Paul showed he was a clever orator by picking this unusual local dedication as the starting point of his arguments. However, there are no archaeological traces anywhere in the Roman world of statues to a single "unknown god." There are several examples, on the other hand, of monuments dedicated to "All the Unknown Gods." Philostratus, the author of the *Life of Apollonius of Tyana* in the early third century, notes that Athens, above all, often raised altars "even to unknown gods." The purpose was to be sure that no local god or goddess was angered by being forgotten or neglected and brought bad fortune to the city. In general, then, the evidence suggests that, although Paul might have found a specific statue to a single unknown god, he more probably adapted the plural inscription to "all unknown gods" in order to make his case for the God of the Jews as the only God for all peoples.

Several people were converted by this message, but most of the worldly philosophical debaters of Athens scoffed at the idea of a resurrection of the dead, and put Paul off, telling him to come back another time and tell them more. They were glad to be rid of him for the day. Paul knew when he had met defeat, and soon left this skeptical city to begin his ministry at Corinth.

Chapter 15

PAUL'S MINISTRY IN CORINTH

Corinth, like Athens, was a major cultural and commercial metropolis of the Mediterranean world. Situated at the very northern edge of the Peloponnesian peninsula at the one crossing point from mainland Greece, so that it controlled all traffic between the north and south of the country, and at the same time placed centrally between two deep isthmuses that jutted in from the Adriatic Sea on the west and from the Aegean Sea on the east, it was ideally located to control the major ship traffic from Rome to the east. Strabo, the Roman geographer, called it "the crossroads of the world." Homer, in his *Iliad*, and other ancient writers referred to Corinth mostly with the adjective "wealthy." The city was ancient—traces of early settlement go back to the fifth millennium BC! Because of its key location, it was often attacked, and relied on its steep citadel, the 1500-foot-high hill of the Acrocorinth, and very extensive walls to protect itself. Its most traumatic defeat came in 146 BC when it joined in the revolt against Rome, and the admiral Lucius Mummius leveled the city and deported all of its inhabitants. Cicero visited the site sixty-five years later in 79 to 77 BC and found it mostly ruins. It remained a mere village until restored by Julius Caesar in 44 BC. Strabo tells us that the new settlers were mostly freed slaves who brought their many skills and their new freedom to make it quickly into a powerful commercial center once again. So the city that Paul saw was relatively new and filled with impressive Roman public works.

The key to Corinth's wealth was its control of shipping across the Mediterranean. The rather small and fragile merchant ships in use had to stay relatively close to the shoreline in order to seek quick protection in sheltered bays if bad weather arose. Many ships were often lost in the rough seas and storms around the bottom of the Peloponnesus in particular. Crossing the narrow

land neck at Corinth instead saved perhaps a week of travel and avoided the danger from storms. As early as Homer, people dreamed of cutting a canal across the mere four miles of land separating the two isthmuses, but it never happened. Instead, Periander, the Corinthian ruler about 600 BC, built an overland paved road with grooved tracks to transport the boats from one side to the other. As a result, the city developed two harbors: Lechaeum facing west, and Cenchreae facing east to the Aegean. Boats would come up to the end of the isthmus from either side, unload the cargo from their boats onto carts, and drag the ships across the two miles of land to the other isthmus, reload the cargo, and sail on into the opposite sea, saving hundreds of miles of dangerous coastal journey around the Peloponnesus and days of travel, for the small price of a tax to the Corinthian city-state.

As a result, Corinth was a wild seaport town with all of the vices and pleasures sailors expected after long sea voyages. Aristophanes invented a verb, "to Corinthasize," meaning "to fornicate." Plato called all prostitutes "Corinthian girls," and Strabo claimed (probably exaggeratedly) that the city had a thousand prostitutes. At the same time, the city was the hub of culture and arts for the lower half of Greece. It was filled with rich homes and stately public buildings and temples, as well as the highest and most protected acropolis in all of Greece that served as a fortress of last resort in time of siege. It was also the capital of the province of Achaia, with a proconsul appointed by the Roman senate. And it was the home of the Isthmian Games, held every two years in the spring at the shrine of Poseidon. Paul could have attended the games in 51 AD, and he certainly was aware of the games since his first use of athletic imagery for the Christian life comes in 1 Corinthians 9:24–27. Although the ruins of Corinth that remain today are impressive, there are no known remnants of the Jewish community and its synagogue yet discovered.

When Paul arrived at Corinth, about the year 51 AD, he was fortunate to meet another newly arriving Christian couple, Priscilla (or Prisca) and Aquila, who had just been expelled from Rome by an edict of the emperor Claudius after the riots stirred up against Christians by the Jewish community in 49 AD. Aquila, like Paul, was a tentmaker by profession, and the two entered into business together to support themselves for however long their stay might be. It turned out to be one of the longest stays that Paul spent voluntarily anyplace during his ministry, eighteen months. Paul was able to speak about his message of Jesus as Messiah in the synagogue on the Sabbath for a while, until a majority forced him to stop. He quickly moved next door from the synagogue to the house of a Gentile God-fearer, Titius Justus. And there, as he had done in the other cities of Greece, he began to proclaim his message directly to the Gentiles. Paul was not without Jewish supporters as well. The head of the synagogue, Crispus, became a believer in Jesus along with his entire family. But Paul's foes in the Jewish community could not accept his success in winning followers while preaching from the house right next door to the Jewish center for the city. They brought a court case against him to Gallio, the proconsul who governed the city, but as had the officials in Thessalonica, Gallio refused to treat the case as a crime, seeing it as an inner-Jewish dispute instead.

Paul continued to preach in Corinth for many months more before deciding it was time to move on. He set sail first to Ephesus and later traveled down to Jerusalem before eventually returning to his home base at Antioch. Thus he brought to a close what is universally known as his Second Missionary Journey (Acts 15:36 to 18:22).

Chapter 16

PAUL AND HIS DISCIPLES

St. Paul never traveled alone on his missionary journeys. The Acts of the Apostles reports that right from the beginning of his work, "The Holy Spirit said, 'Set apart for me Barnabas and Saul for the work to which I have called them'" (Acts 13:2). He traveled with Barnabas and Barnabas's nephew, John Mark, for the entire first missionary effort in Acts 13–14. Mark apparently did not want to go with Paul on the second missionary journey, and so Paul separated from Barnabas and Mark and instead chose Silas to go with him (Acts 15:40), and soon added Timothy as well (Acts 16:1–4). But later Mark must have returned to Paul, for he is mentioned as a companion again in 2 Timothy 4:11; Colossians 4:11; and Philemon 24. In the middle of the account of this second journey, Luke stops narrating that "Paul did this," or "he did that" and begins to say "we." This "firsthand journal" suddenly appears when Paul leaves Asia and takes a ship to begin his work in Greece in Acts 16:11: "We set sail from Troas and went directly to Samothrace." Whether Luke himself accompanied Paul and wrote his own notes or was using the notes of another companion of Paul, we cannot know, but clearly Luke had access to direct knowledge of Paul's travels.

Why did Paul not work alone? We get two clues from the New Testament itself. One comes from Luke's account of Paul's stay in Lystra in Acts 14:8–18. When Paul cured a woman fortune-teller of her evil spirit, the crowds wanted to worship Barnabas as the god Zeus and Paul as the god Hermes, the messenger of Zeus, "because he was their chief spokesman" (Acts 14:12). The second clue comes from Paul's practice of sending his associates back to check on the churches where he had preached to make sure all was well. In 2 Corinthians 8:16–24 he discusses Titus's mission to that church, and in Philippians 2:19–30 he mentions sending Timothy and Epaphroditus to that church. When Paul is

forced to go on to Athens from Thessalonica and Beroea in Acts 17, he leaves Timothy and Silas behind to support the work he had just begun. Thus Paul depended heavily on his associates to make his preaching successful. Alone he could never have been able to found so many new communities and continue to guide them as they grew and often suffered persecution.

One sign of Paul's deep respect for the contributions his associates and companions made to his ministry is the number of letters he wrote in partnership with one of them. 1 and 2 Thessalonians are sent from "Paul, Silvanus, and Timothy"; 1 Corinthians is from "Paul and Sosthenes"; 2 Corinthians is from "Paul and Timothy," as are also the Letters to the Philippians, Colossians, and Philemon. Many scholars identify Paul's co-letter-writer Sosthenes with the leader of the synagogue opposed to Paul in Corinth who is named in Acts 18:12–17. It is thought he converted and served with Paul.

In all, Paul names these and other associates throughout his letters. Besides those we have already discussed, he refers to Apollos as a fellow apostle in Acts 18:24–27 and 1 Corinthians 1:10; 3:3–6; 4:6–8; Titus 3:13; Tychicus in Acts 20:4; Ephesians 6:21–22; Colossians 4:7; 2 Timothy 4:12; Titus 3:12; Luke the "beloved physician" in Colossians 4:14; Philemon 24; and 2 Timothy 4:11; Crescens in 2 Timothy 4:10; Titus in Galatians 2:1–3; 2 Corinthians 2:13; 7:6, 13; 8:6, 16–17, 23; 12:18; 2 Timothy 4:10; Titus 1:4; Demas in Philemon 24; Aristarchus in Colossians 4:14; Philemon 24; Artemas in Titus 3:12; Trophimus in 2 Timothy 4:20; Onesimus in Colossians 4:9; Philemon 10; Jesus Justus in Colossians 4:11; and Epaphras in Colossians 1:7; 4:12; Philemon 23.

The best-known of Paul's companions were Aquila and Priscilla (or Prisca), who had been driven out of Rome by the Emperor Claudius in 49 AD during a Jewish uprising there. Paul met them as they were both arriving in Corinth, and they lived and worked together as tentmakers there for eighteen months in Acts 18:1–3. Later the two traveled with Paul to Ephesus in Acts 18:18–19; converted Apollos in Acts 18:24–28; and, when they had returned home to Rome, received Paul's greetings in Romans 16:3; 1 Corinthians 16:19; 2 Timothy 4:19.

Chapter 17

PAUL'S LETTERS

One of the unique features of the New Testament is that it contains many letters to the various new Christian communities. The Old Testament has no such collection of letters among its books. These letters add a dimension that cannot be found in the great narrative stories of the Gospels and Acts of the Apostles, or in the Book of Revelation. They give us a glimpse into the daily questions and problems faced by new Christians who are trying to understand and live out the new faith in Christ that they have received. Letters mostly address difficult issues that have arisen from misunderstanding the message of the apostles, or from efforts of individuals to have things their own way.

   The collection of letters makes up about one-third of the entire New Testament. There are three letters attributed to the apostle John, two to St. Peter, one to James, and one to Jude. But by far the largest number of letters is attributed to Paul, fourteen in all out of the total of twenty-one. Moreover, his words are the earliest record of the Christian message, even earlier than our written Gospels, which were not composed until perhaps 65 to 90 AD. Scholars generally agree that at least seven were certainly written by Paul himself, or dictated by him: Romans, 1 Corinthians, 2 Corinthians, Galatians, Philippians, Philemon, and 1 Thessalonians. Most scholars would also accept Colossians and 2 Thessalonians, but many doubt whether Paul himself, rather than his disciples, wrote Ephesians, 1 and 2 Timothy, and Titus. Hebrews is attributed to Paul by tradition, but nowhere claims to be of Paul, and certainly was not written by him. First Thessalonians is the earliest letter, written perhaps in 51 AD. The last letter from Paul himself probably could not have been after 64 (or perhaps 67) AD, when he was martyred in Rome. And the last dates for letters that may have been written by his followers, such as 1 and 2 Timothy, would be in the 90s AD. The letter that would qualify as Paul's final message, if one accepts it as genuine, is 2 Timothy. It is filled with personal information and poignant details about his expected death. He has been left alone except for Luke, and feels abandoned. But as the winter approaches he asks that Timothy provide his heavy cloak and his books that he had left behind.

The collection of Ephesians, Colossians, Philippians, and Philemon is commonly called the "Captivity Epistles" because Paul notes in each of them that he is a prisoner. Titus and 1 and 2 Timothy are called the "Pastoral Epistles" because they deal with direct advice to individual church leaders.

In general, these letters are a great treasure for knowing the early church. Unlike the cultures behind the Old Testament in which most people could not read or write, the world of Paul benefited from the widespread emphasis in Greek and Roman society on the education of both men and women in reading and writing. In the two centuries after Jesus, we have thousands of letters that have survived from places all over the Roman Empire, written by ordinary people about ordinary issues of their daily life. They allow us to understand the way people really lived and what they thought and how they coped with problems. Paul's intense and very direct manner of responding to the questions of his new communities in his letters gives us that same insight into the first decades of Christianity.

Chapter 18

PAUL WRITES TO THE GALATIANS

Galatia was the scene of Paul's earliest missionary work when he went to Perga, Iconium, Lystra, and Derbe on his First Missionary Journey (Acts 14). They were all in the southern part of the province, but later he also visited the northern areas on his Second and Third Missionary Journeys (Acts 16:6 and 18:23). Scholars do not agree on whether the Letter to the Galatians in the New Testament was written back to the first group in the south, perhaps about 49 or 50 AD, or later to the northern converts, likely around 54 or 55 AD. He mentions his meeting with the leading apostles in Jerusalem in chapter 2, which probably took place about 49 AD, so the letter would have to come after that event. But in favor of the later dating of the letter, Paul also mentions his confrontation with Peter that happened sometime after the apostolic council because Peter went back on the agreement that Gentile converts would not have to become Jews but would be treated equally to Jewish converts. Paul's words are forceful and determined on this point: "I opposed Cephas [Peter's Aramaic name] to his face because he was certainly wrong! Indeed, before some people came from James, he used to eat with the Gentiles, but when they arrived, he withdrew and separated himself because he was afraid of the Jewish party" (Gal 2:11–12). Paul was particularly upset since it meant that Jewish Christians were once again insisting that all Gentiles had to become Jews first. This violated the entire Gospel message that Paul preached. So he boldly addressed Peter on this issue: "I said to Cephas in front of all, 'If you, although a Jew, live like a Gentile and not like a Jew, how can you insist that Gentiles live like Jews?'" (Gal 2:14).

Paul devotes two-thirds of his Letter to the Galatians (chaps. 1–4) to showing that the Law by itself cannot bring salvation to Jew or to Gentile.

Salvation comes only by faith in God's saving power first given in the promises to Abraham and the ancestors before there even was a Moses and the Law. Christ has now brought the Promise to both Jewish converts, by fulfilling their messianic hope, and to Gentile converts, by the grace of the Holy Spirit. In Christ, God has granted both the forgiveness from sin and the gift of everlasting life. So Christians should rejoice in this freedom in Christ. As Paul says, "For freedom Christ has set us free and so do not ever go back under the yoke of slavery again" (Gal 5:1). He ends his advice in chapters 5 and 6 with a rich description of what the spiritual life of a Christian should be. In all, it is Paul's most impassioned letter because he saw his very mission to bring the Gospel to all the pagan nations at stake.

Chapter 19

PAUL WRITES TO THE CORINTHIANS

We know that Paul kept very close to his new community of Christians in Corinth. He wrote at least two major letters back to them which have become part of the New Testament, and mentions other letters that he sent which have long since been lost or made part of the current Second Letter to the Corinthians in our Bible (see 2 Cor 2:3–4, 9; 10:10). Because Corinth was such an unruly city, it could be expected that many of his converts were also strong-willed and argumentative over just about everything. Paul's First Letter to the Corinthians may have been written when he spent a short time in Ephesus on his way back to Antioch at the end of his Second Missionary Journey, but more likely it was during his Third Missionary Journey, when he stayed at Ephesus for two years (see the hints in 1 Cor 16:7–8). In any case, he received regular reports from his associates who traveled to his churches for him, like Sosthenes, whom he mentions in the opening of his letter (1 Cor 1:1), or from members of the congregation who visited Ephesus, such as Stephanas, Fortunatus, and Achaicus, whom he tells the Corinthians had recently arrived (1 Cor 16:17). Paul dealt with some doctrinal problems, such as their questions about the resurrection of the dead (1 Cor 15), or the nature of spiritual gifts (1 Cor 12 and 14), but for the most part he had more practical matters on his mind. He had received alarming accounts of how some Corinthians were quarreling about which faction was the more Christian, and some claimed they had more superior wisdom of Christ than others, and yet others were bringing members of the community to the Roman law courts, or living in forbidden sexual unions, or even participating in pagan festivals. Their Eucharist was especially divided, with the rich refusing to share with the poorer members of the community. Paul deals with each of these divisive issues, trying to bring unity and humility back to this community. The letter is one of the best windows into the life of the early church and the many struggles its members endured while figuring out what being a Christian really meant. Paul draws a profound picture of the community as the body of Christ in chapter 12, and his description of the community living by love in chapter 13 is considered one of the greatest passages he ever wrote. Even to this day, it is the favorite description of Christian marriage, used in perhaps half of all wedding ceremonies. He lays out both what love is and is not, but at its heart, it is always thinking and acting for the good of the other person and never for oneself first.

His Second Letter to the Corinthians is perhaps the single most powerfully written letter Paul composed. It frequently employs the Greek classical rhetorical style of the diatribe, which employs series of questions and challenges thrown at the audience, paradoxical twists and reversals found in his own ministry experience, and the insistence on his authority. The letter is a defense of his ministry to them and thus his right to insist on certain behavior from them. It reveals the close working relationship that Paul had with his associates, in this case, with Titus (chapter 7), and gives a moving picture of his own sufferings and burdens endured in preaching the Gospel (chapters 11 and 12), as well as a persuasive argument for giving generously to the collection for the mother church in Jerusalem (chapter 8). The date of its composition is unknown, but it must have followed sometime after First Corinthians, perhaps around 58 AD.

Chapter 20

PAUL AND THE SPIRIT

In the Acts of the Apostles, Luke stresses that the early church was specially marked by the action of the Holy Spirit. Jesus promises that the disciples would receive the Spirit in Acts 1:8; it descends upon them in the upper room in Acts 2:1–3; it leads to Peter and the apostles boldly proclaiming Christ in Acts 2:4–5, 33; and then it is poured out on the new converts in Acts 2:38; 4:8; 6:8; 9:17; 13:52; and 19:1–7. The first deacon-martyr, Stephen, is filled with "faith and the Holy Spirit" in Acts 6:5. And the Spirit guides the decisions of the church leaders in Acts 13:2; 15:28; and 20:28. Thus, for Luke, the entire response and bold preaching of the Gospel is made possible for the first Christians by the work of the Holy Spirit that Christ had promised them.

St. Paul himself speaks of the Holy Spirit throughout his letters. As in Acts, it is seen as a dynamic force from God, sent by Christ, and is not always clearly yet understood, at this early stage, to be a person of the Trinity equal to Father and Son. The church would need nearly three hundred years until the great Councils of Nicea and Constantinople in 325 and 381, to define the Trinity so sharply. But Paul never separates the Spirit from the Father's saving action for humankind nor from Christ's risen power for the believer. It is intimately associated with both Father and Christ in all of Paul's writings. For Paul, the Spirit unites us with Christ—there is one spirit for those who cling to the Lord (1 Cor 6:17), and the new covenant in Christ confers a new spirit on the believer (2 Cor 3:6, 8). The Spirit also grants us adoption by God with Christ (Rom 8:16; Gal 4:6) so that we become the temple of the Holy Spirit in our lives (1 Cor 3:16; 6:19; 8:11). By this adoption with Christ nothing can separate us ever again from the love of God (Rom 8:38–39).

In turn, possession of the Holy Spirit means that we are given the power to live out our Christian commitment with Christ. The Spirit enables us to pray (Rom 8:15; 1 Cor 12:3); and it searches out the deep things of God (1 Cor 2:10–16); and those who live in the Spirit must walk in the Spirit (Gal 5:25). And the Spirit is the principle of love for all believers (Rom 5:5; Col 1:8; Gal 5:13–26). But perhaps the most famous expressions of the Spirit for Paul is in the spiritual gifts that the believers receive to build up the daily life of the community as the "Body of Christ." Paul treats these spiritual gifts in depth in Romans 12 and 1 Corinthians 12 and 14. They serve to give witness to the presence of the risen Christ in the church and to the firm conviction of our hope of life in Christ. In Romans 12, Paul asserts we are all part of the one body of Christ but yet individual members with our own unique roles to play, and some are given gifts of prophecy, or ministering, or teaching, or leading, or exhorting others. Whatever the gift, the person must use it at the service of the church.

In 1 Corinthians 12, Paul makes the analogy again that we are all part of one body but each a different part of that body. No one could act alone, thinking that he or she is the only important part; nor should one gift be considered greater than other gifts. In this chapter he names the spiritual gifts of apostles, prophets, teachers, miracle workers, healers, assistants, administrators, and those who speak in tongues or interpret tongues. In 1 Corinthians 14, Paul particularly discusses the gifts of prophecy and speaking in tongues. They are both good for building up the church in faith, but prophecy is superior to tongues because, as Paul says, "Tongues build up the speaker, but prophecy builds up the church" (1 Cor 14:4). If one speaks in tongues, it is good, but the speaker should also seek to be able to interpret and explain his tongues, for Paul insists he would rather speak five intelligible words of instruction than ten thousand words in tongues (1 Cor 14:19). He concludes by saying that the Corinthians should seek the gift of prophecy, allow the gift of tongues, but above all, make sure all of it is kept within orderly bounds that inspires and uplifts the congregation and does not lead to personal rivalries and disorder.

Chapter 21

PAUL'S THIRD MISSIONARY JOURNEY: TROAS

The Third Missionary Journey is narrated in Acts 18:23 to 20:38. We do not know how long Paul remained in Antioch, but Luke suggests it was only a short time. For within the next verse, after getting home, Paul was off again, passing through the cities of his First Missionary Journey in south-central Turkey in order to visit the provinces of Galatia and Phrygia (Acts 18:23). Somewhat later he continued on to Ephesus where he spent some time with the disciples who had never been fully taught about Jesus. They had received the baptism of John the Baptist for repentance, but had never heard about receiving the Holy Spirit in the Christian baptism. Paul baptized them, and immediately they were filled with the charismatic gifts of the Spirit and began speaking in tongues and prophesying (Acts 19:1–7). Altogether, Paul spent three months preaching there in the local synagogue before Jewish opponents forced him out. As he had done in Corinth, Paul simply moved to a public lecture hall, the house of Tyrannus, and for over two more years stayed in Ephesus proclaiming his Gospel to the Gentiles, winning many converts (Acts 19:10). He became well known in the city for his powers of healing the sick and driving out evil spirits. But when others tried to make money using Jesus' name as magic, they were attacked by the very evil spirits they were seeking to remove.

Paul was planning to move on and return through the cities of Greece once more before going again to Jerusalem. He was even considering a first visit to Rome (Acts 19:21). But suddenly a riot was stirred up against him, not by the Jewish leaders, but by the pagan silver makers who made small medals of the goddess Artemis for worshipers to bring to her temple. Paul's success at conversions was hurting their business badly, and they wanted to drive Paul out. In the end, the city magistrates were able to calm the crowd and dismiss them, but Paul knew he had to leave quickly. So he departed to Macedonia (Philippi and Thessalonica) and down to Corinth for a three-month stay (Acts 20:2–3). Then reversing his steps, he went back up to Philippi again, and sailed back to the Asian coast to Troas, about two hundred miles north of Ephesus.

Paul stayed with his disciples in Troas for seven days, and on that Sunday, when the Christians were gathered to "break the bread" (Acts 20:7), Paul gave such a long sermon into the night that a young man named Eutychus fell asleep in his window perch and fell three stories to his death. Paul revived him and gave him over to his friends, and then calmly returned to the upper room to finish the Eucharist and continue talking until dawn! He had much to say to them since he was leaving for Miletus the next morning and was quite conscious that he might never see them again.

Chapter 22

PAUL WRITES TO ROME

Sometime while in Greece on his Third Missionary Journey, most likely during his three-month stay at Corinth, Paul composed and sent a very lengthy letter to the church of Rome to prepare the way for his visit there. This letter probably dates, therefore, between 56 and 58 AD. It is unlike any other letter he wrote, since this was not to a church that he had founded. As a result, he did not answer particular questions that members of the local church had written to him or address problems that had been reported to him. Instead he laid out carefully the description of the Gospel that he preached in order to reassure these Roman Christians who did not know him but may have heard of him as one who was not fully orthodox. Their suspicions may well have originated in stories about his conflicts with Jewish-Christian groups over the admission of Gentiles into the church. He certainly stresses to the Romans that he was appointed by the Holy Spirit to the special role as an apostle to Gentiles above all (Rom 15:14–21). Paul tells the Romans that he had longed to visit them for some time to complete his preaching to the Gentiles there as well (Rom 1:10–14). He had been prevented for some reason (Rom 15:22), but now he has been able to plan it since he had completed his work in the areas of Asia and Greece and saw no more opportunities in those regions (Rom 15:23). He also hoped to go to Spain and to have the Roman church sponsor his mission there after he had stayed with them awhile (Rom 15:24). But he will be some time coming since, before he could journey to Rome, he must bring the collection of money for their poor to the church in Jerusalem.

Paul may have learned much about the church of Rome from his friends Aquila and Priscilla, who had been exiled from Rome by the emperor Claudius in 49 AD and with whom he had lived in Corinth as tentmakers after the couple

had arrived as exiles. The emperor had ordered the expulsion of specific Jews because of arguments over a certain "Chrestus." This was surely a mirror of the violent disputes that Paul had faced in the synagogues in Thessalonica and elsewhere over whether Jesus was the Christ ("Messiah"). It also means that the Christian community was already strongly present in Rome before Paul ever came there. We do not know which apostle founded the church in Rome, but it would not be surprising that it happened very early on, since it was the capital of the Empire and, as the Romans said, "All roads lead to Rome." Paul names a great number of people whom he had met or knew about in his final chapter, 16, so he had been well informed about the situation in Rome.

His letter is intended to show that the Gospel he preaches is compatible with what they had been taught, and so, for example, he cites the Old Testament more often than in his other letters. But he also needed to provide the arguments as to why Gentiles have been called to have an equal place in the community with the Jewish converts. He lays out his familiar message that being faithful to the Law alone was not enough to save Jews, no less Gentiles, for they also needed *faith* in God's unique and only-now-revealed plan to deliver human beings from their sins through the death and resurrection of Jesus. God's plan also promised everlasting life with the risen Jesus to those who were united with him by this faith. Paul clearly spoke to a church that was made up of both Jewish and Gentile members—but who were not yet in agreement on the question whether the Gentile converts had to also embrace Judaism's major practices. This Jewish-Gentile question is also reflected in chapters 9 through 11 with his tortured and passionate treatment of how those Jews who had not become Christian would also continue to enjoy God's covenant promise, and some day be united with the Gentile Christians.

His major argument for salvation in Christ is presented in chapters 1 through 8. It proceeds in four steps: (1) in chapters 1:16—3:20 he argues that all humans are subject to sin and therefore death, whether Jew or Gentile; (2) in chapters 3:21—5:21 he explains why faith in Christ alone is necessary for freedom from sin; (3) in chapters 6:1—7:25 he lays out what freedom from sin and the Law in Christ will mean for believers; and (4) in chapter 8:1–39 he describes the power of the Holy Spirit to transform and conform us to the love of God in union with Christ, which will guarantee our everlasting life with God. Paul's powerful description of God's love for us in 8:28–39 is perhaps the finest passage in all of his letters!

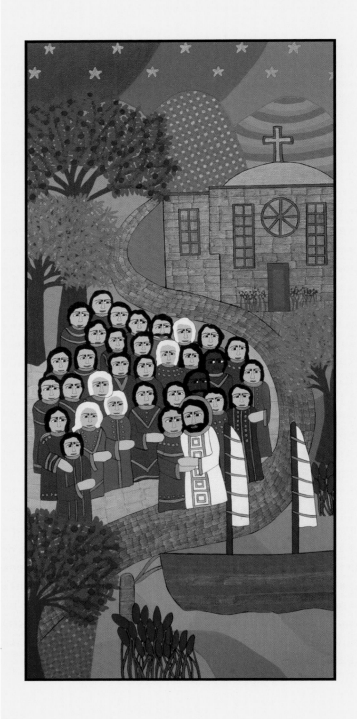

Chapter 23

FAREWELL AT MILETUS

We left Paul before the last chapter of the Letter to the Romans in Troas near the end of his Third Missionary Journey. From its beginning at Acts 18:23, Paul had left Antioch and traveled through all of Turkey to Ephesus, where he stayed for nearly three years before continuing on through Macedonia and Greece and back again the same route. From Troas, however, he decided against stopping at Ephesus, where he was so well known, but proceeded to the nearby port of Miletus to make his final farewells. He asked the elders of Ephesus to meet him there for a quick good-bye so that he would not miss a ship leaving for Palestine and the port of Caesarea that would get him to Jerusalem in time for Pentecost (Acts 20:13–16). Luke provides us with the lengthy farewell address of Paul to these church leaders whom he had come to know so well in his long stay among them. It goes from Acts 20:17 to 20:35. He tells the elders clearly that he was not going to Jerusalem simply on his own whim, but that he had received strong promptings of the Holy Spirit that he must go there, although he would certainly be persecuted and arrested if he did. Indeed, he was convinced he would never again see his churches in the area of Ephesus (called by the Romans the province of Asia). But, just as he knew he was destined to suffer for the Gospel when he reached the holy city, they too must be prepared for suffering. He warns them that they would soon be perse-cuted as leaders of the local church and find that "wolves," heretical teachers, would try to lead the people astray. Yet they should count on the grace of Christ to enlighten and strengthen them in these challenges, even as Paul had always done. He closes with giving his own example as the defense of his min-istry. He had always worked with his own hands to support himself the whole time he ministered to them, no doubt by his tent-making skills. He did so to encourage others to always give to the poor and support the weak. In this all Christians would fulfill the Lord's words, "It is more blessed to give than to receive." The quotation actually comes from Sirach 4:31, one of the Deutero-canonical books of the Old Testament, but Luke clearly considers it inspired by God and therefore attributes the saying to the risen Jesus as God's Son.

Acts 21 gives us a wonderful account of how a sea voyage was taken in Roman times. Paul had to change ships many times as he made his way along the coastline from port to port, often being able to stay a week here and four days there before the next ship was available to go in the direction they wanted. Paul goes from Miletus to the islands of Cos and Rhodes and Patara. They then sailed along the southern coast of Cyprus for protection against storms, followed by a dash across the open ocean to reach the Phoenician port of Tyre. Another boat took them down the coast to Ptolemais, and a final short trip brought them to Caesarea, the capital of Roman Palestine. From there the trip to Jerusalem would be overland. But at each port the Christians with whom they stayed received charismatic prophecies of the Spirit that Paul would face arrest and prison if he went to Jerusalem, and they begged him both at Tyre and at Caesarea not to go there. But Paul would not be persuaded, and Luke tells us that those with him simply gave up and joined him in prayer that God's will be done (Acts 21:12).

Chapter 24

PAUL, A PRISONER IN JERUSALEM

Although Paul was warmly received by the church in Jerusalem when he arrived, James and the elders were worried that the crowds of devout Jews who had come up for the celebration of Pentecost would certainly discover that he was the one who had led many Jews to follow Jesus and to join with Gentiles who were not bound to keep the Law. Acts 21:15–26 explains how they devised a plan to protect Paul from any accusers. They had Paul pay the fees for the purification rites for some of their men who had made a vow in the Temple. Thus Paul would prove he was himself a faithful Jew. At the same time, the elders reinforced their regulations, first agreed upon with Paul in the Council of Jerusalem recorded in Acts 15, that Gentile converts must respect Jewish observances and customs.

It almost worked. Paul followed all the proper rites right up to the last of the seven days before some Jews who had also come from Asia recognized him and stirred up a riot against him. Paul was dragged by a crowd out of the Temple grounds and beaten until the Roman tribune rushed up to stop the trouble. Thinking Paul was an Egyptian insurgent and not being able to get a clear picture of why the crowd was beating on him, he had Paul arrested and brought to the Roman barracks. Because Paul could speak Greek fluently he convinced the tribune to let him address the crowds that had followed them to the barracks.

From this point forward, Luke constructs an elaborate series of discussions between Paul and various Jewish and Roman parties. This takes up all of chapters 22 to 26 and sets the stage for Paul's being sent to Rome as the final act of the Book of Acts. In Acts 22 he first addresses the Jewish crowds that had attacked him and explains his conversion and mission to proclaim the Gospel of Jesus to the Gentiles. The crowd just got angrier, and so the tribune brought

Paul into the prison. But when he found out that Paul was a Roman citizen, he decided to have him confront the entire Jewish Sanhedrin. Acts 23 records that meeting. The high priest wants him condemned, but Paul turns the argument away from himself by announcing that he was being persecuted over the question of the resurrection of the dead. Among the Sanhedrin members, this was a belief strongly held by Pharisees but just as strongly denied by the Sadducees, and the two parties got into a shouting and shoving match that forced the tribune to stop the proceedings. When a plot to kill Paul is uncovered, the tribune finally decides to send Paul back to Caesarea under heavy guard to have his case decided by the Roman governor Felix himself. The governor, however, is uncertain of what to do, and decides to send for the high priest and Jewish leaders to present their case a second time.

Chapter 25

PAUL SAILS FOR ROME

Chapters 24 through 26 of Acts cover Paul's imprisonment in Caesarea for over two years under two governors, Felix and Festus. Despite the new charges brought by the priests against Paul, Felix recognized that they were trumped up and refused to condemn Paul. On the other hand, he wanted to keep favor with the Jews over whom he ruled, and so he did not release Paul but kept him in a loose "house arrest" for the remainder of his term in office (Acts 24:24–27). When his successor, Porcius Festus, took over as governor, the Jews renewed their charges, and Festus held a trial. Being new in the role, he was even more concerned about keeping the Jewish leaders from stirring up trouble than Felix had been. He also realized the charges were weak, but yielded to the Jewish demands that Paul be tried in Jerusalem. Paul found out that they planned to kill him on the road, so he exercised his right as a Roman citizen to appeal over the local courts and have his trial heard before the imperial courts in Rome (Acts 25:11–12). Festus agreed to this, but did not know what he could charge Paul with that would require such a trial in Rome. So he asked King Herod Agrippa and his wife Bernice to listen to Paul and tell him what grounds he could use for the indictment.

Paul's defense before Agrippa allows Luke to present the third separate account of Paul's conversion on the road to Damascus. In a very cleverly constructed speech, Paul praises the king as an expert in Jewish Law, and then presents his own past as a zealous defender of Judaism and servant of the high priest in the persecution of Christians. He then recounts the direct command from Jesus in his heavenly vision to preach the repentance of sin to Jews and to bring the Gentiles out of darkness into the light of the faith. Paul then supports this mission by appealing to the prophets who looked forward to a Messiah who would have to suffer as he brought salvation to Jew and Gentile alike. All of what Paul says would be acceptable to Jews who believed in a coming Messiah. The only difficult hurdle was the claim that the Messiah must suffer to accomplish his mission. Most Jews looked forward instead to the Messiah as a triumphant king who would restore the peace and glory of David's ancient kingdom. At the end of Paul's impassioned speech Agrippa can find no fault in him and would have recommended setting him free. But because he had appealed to the emperor, Paul must now go to Rome.

Chapter 26

PAUL, SHIPWRECKED IN MALTA

Luke reports Paul's journey by sea to Rome in remarkable detail, as though he were copying from a log kept by someone on the trip. He frequently repeats, *"we* did this" or *"we* departed from here" and similar "we" phrases that suggest he was drawing from the written diary of someone who accompanied Paul on many of his missionary journeys since the same "we" passages occur in chapters 16, 20, and 21. Just before they start, Acts 15:40 says Paul chose Silas to be his companion on his journeys, so it is possible that Silas kept the diary. But it could also have been Luke himself, although we do not know if he was with Paul on these trips or not.

They sailed first on a ship bound for ports in the Roman province of Asia, that is, along the Turkish coast. So they went from Caesarea up the Palestinian coast to Sidon, where they stayed for several days, and Paul visited friends. Then they crossed the sea to Cyprus and stayed close to its southern coast until, at the end of the island, they crossed over to the Turkish coast at Myra in Lycia. Here the centurion in charge of Paul as a prisoner found a ship that was going directly to Italy. But the winds were against them, and the ship had to struggle to reach the end of the Turkish peninsula at Cnidus, and then across the open ocean to Crete, and very slowly along the coast of Crete to a port called "Fair Havens" (Acts 27:8). It was so late in the autumn now that sea voyages were dangerous in the face of winter storms. Paul had a vision that the ship would meet disaster, but the centurion was determined to go on and the ship's captain wanted to proceed, so off they sailed. They hoped to find a better port to spend the winter at Phoenix, on the western end of Crete. But once at sea, a hurricane struck hard and mercilessly drove the ship off course for fourteen days. The crew threw most of the gear and cargo overboard, and

feared the ship itself was going to sink. At that point, Paul had another vision that the ship's crew would all be saved, and soon they found the water getting shallower. The sailors were conspiring to escape and leave the soldiers and their prisoners to die on board when the ship crashed into rocks on shore. Paul warned the centurion about the plot, and he cut loose the lifeboat so no one could leave. The ship soon ran aground on a sandbar, and somehow everyone made it to shore (Acts 27:39–44).

The people of the island treated the survivors well and fed and built a fire for them. While gathering firewood, Paul was bitten by a poisonous snake. The local people reacted by observing that suffering such a terrible fate after escaping death at sea must prove he really was a murderer. But they were soon amazed that it had no effect on him at all, and instead began to think he might be a god (Acts 28:1–6). Their winter refuge turned out to be the island of Malta.

Chapter 27

PAUL ARRIVES IN ROME

The party spent the winter months in Malta. Their first stay was at the estate of Publius, the chief official of the island. While there, Paul cured his son of his chronic illness through prayer, and soon everyone was bringing their sick for Paul to heal. Altogether, they stayed three months on Malta, and when a ship was found headed for Rome, the people brought all kinds of provisions for Paul and his party and wished them a safe journey.

The final sea voyage from Malta to Rome was uneventful. They sailed across to Syracuse in Sicily, and then around the toe of the boot of Italy to Rhegium, and from there up the west coast to Puteoli, where the Christians welcomed Paul to stay with them for a week. Afterward, they led him overland from there to Rome. Many of the Roman Christians came out to the Appian Way to meet Paul and his party, and accompanied him into Rome. The Roman officials allowed Paul to rent a place to stay on his own, and merely assigned a soldier to be on guard at the house.

Paul's first action, according to Acts 28:17–29, was to ask to see the leaders of the *Jewish* synagogue and explain that he was not in prison as their enemy but because he had appealed to Rome when Jewish leaders in Jerusalem had opposed his being released. The Roman Jewish Community had heard he was among the believers in Jesus, but no one had denounced his work or warned against receiving him, so they invited him to speak in the synagogue. When he delivered his arguments for Jesus as the Messiah, some were convinced and some were opposed, but the synagogue as a whole would not support him. So Paul decided to work elsewhere. Quoting Isaiah 6:9 about Israel's inability to see and understand, he clearly announced that from then on he would preach only to the Gentiles in Rome. Acts ends its accounts of Paul's missionary life by saying: "For two full years Paul remained in his rented quarters and welcomed all who came to him. With complete boldness and no obstacles at all, he preached about the Kingdom of God and the Lord Jesus Christ" (Acts 28:30–31).

Chapter 28

PAUL MEETS PETER IN ROME (OR DID HE?)

The only time we know for sure that Paul spent in Rome are the two years he lived under house arrest reported in Acts 28. Did Paul ever meet Peter while in Rome? Whether he worked with Peter during this time or not is very uncertain, as we noted above. It is more than possible that the two apostles were never in the city at the same time before the days of their martyrdom under Nero. A number of legends grew up, of course, connecting them together in the city, but no one knows what authenticity they have. For example, one Roman legend reports that the two apostles spent their last days before martyrdom chained in the same prison next to the Roman Forum, which is known today as the Mamertine Prison.

Later tradition did wonder why Luke ended the Acts of the Apostles with Paul apparently not under serious threat for his life. Assuming that after two years of captivity he would be freed, this supposed new freedom fit into his plan to travel to Spain as a missionary, which had been mentioned in Romans 15:24. Pope Clement in his Letter to the Corinthians, written from Rome in the 80s or 90s, asserted that, "[Paul] taught the right manner of life to the whole world, traveling as far as the western boundary, and when he had given testimony before authorities, ended his earthly career and was taken up into the holy place as the greatest model of patient endurance."

Since the western limits of the Roman Empire were in Spain, many scholars believe Paul actually did get there. If he was freed from prison about the year 60 AD or shortly after, he had about three or four years of ministry left. Besides a time in Spain, there are those who believe he made still another

full tour of his communities in Asia and Greece as well. They place the disputed Letters of Timothy and Titus in this period as evidence for his later years. Thus he would have written his First Letter to Timothy from Macedonia during his final missionary travels, in order to strengthen his associate whom he had left as the bishop over Ephesus. He would have sent the Second Letter to Timothy from his final imprisonment in Rome under Nero, a year or two later. In 2 Timothy, in particular, there are some intriguing hints of Paul's last acts. He mentions the parchments and the cloak left at Troas, and talks about how many disciples had abandoned him and how others were absent, although Luke alone had stayed with him. We cannot be sure that this is the same Luke who wrote the Acts of the Apostles, but church tradition has always believed he is. Finally, in the Letter to Titus from about this same time, he appoints Titus to be the bishop for Crete. Thus, if we take together the three pieces of slim evidence found in the New Testament itself, namely, the mention in the Letter to the Romans about Spain, the inconclusive ending of Acts, and the three Pastoral Epistles, we get a picture of a Paul who did not stay in Rome, but continued his missionary work throughout the Empire. He may have had little time to spend with Peter among the Romans as a result. Moreover, Peter himself may have actually lived for only a very short time in Rome.

Chapter 29

PETER AND PAUL MINISTER IN ROME

At least we know that Paul spent two years in Rome with a certain freedom to minister to the church there and try to win over the Gentiles, as Acts 28:30–31 tells us. But what do we know about St. Peter's presence in Rome? We can begin with the mention of Peter in Paul's Letter to the Galatians. There Paul says that Peter was recognized as the apostle who would serve the Jewish converts as Paul was set aside for the Gentiles (Acts 2:7–8). It suggests Peter was also traveling as a missionary to the many Jewish centers in the Roman cities just as Paul had done. Paul goes on to tell us next that he had confronted Peter in Antioch and pointed out that he lived among the Gentiles as much as Paul did (Gal 2:14). This suggests Peter had left Jerusalem for good and was now on the road for the Gospel. There is no further evidence of Peter's life in the New Testament itself except the tradition that he is the author of the First and Second Letters of Peter. However, the earliest mention of his authorship for these letters comes from the writings of St. Irenaeus after 198 AD. Many scholars think the First Letter of Peter is from the 80s or 90s and reflects a baptismal catechism of the early church. But, on the other hand, there are growing arguments that another early Christian document, the *Didache,* could date from the 60s, and it clearly contains a lengthy catechesis for new converts, so there is no absolute reason why Peter could not have written 1 Peter. In contrast, the Second Letter of Peter seems to look back on the death of the apostles in 3:2 and 4, so it is probably a later letter written by disciples. Another reason to doubt that Peter wrote Second Peter is that it views Paul's writings as already on the level of Scripture in the eyes of the church (3:15–16). Origen (died 254 AD) and Jerome (died 420 AD) both doubted Peter had written the letter.

Outside of the New Testament, Clement of Rome's letter, discussed in the last chapter, is the first solid mention of Peter's permanent presence in Rome at the end of his life. Clement cited the tradition that both Peter and Paul were executed in Rome under Nero. This means both died sometime between 64 and 67 AD. Ignatius of Antioch honored Peter and Paul as the leaders of the Roman church in his Letter to the Romans about the year 116. Papias, a few years later, noted that Mark wrote his Gospel to record Peter's preaching in Rome. Tertullian, in the third century, was the first to note that Peter was crucified. Eusebius, the church historian of the early fourth century AD, wrote that both Peter and Paul died on the same day in 67 AD, but we don't know where he got this information.

It does not seem possible that Peter was in Rome when Paul wrote to the Romans about 58 AD, or Paul would surely have expressed greetings to him as he did to so many individuals of that church in Romans 16. Was he there by 60 or 61 AD, when Paul arrived as a prisoner sent from Festus in Acts 27—28? We don't know that from any source. Acts certainly does not mention it, even though the whole book is structured around the two ministries of Peter (Acts 1—12) and Paul (Acts 13—28); and one might expect that Luke would bring the two together if they were really in Rome at the same time at the end of his work. A rather solid tradition that has been supported by archaeological excavations under the Basilica of St. Peter in Rome is that Peter was crucified at the foot of the Vatican Hill and buried in the cemetery that was on its slopes. This is first mentioned by the Roman priest Caius, who served under Pope Zephyrinus (199–217). The emperor Constantine, after he had declared Christianity a legitimate religion of the Empire, went to extraordinary lengths to level the top of the Vatican Hill, and thereby desecrated the cemetery that was there, something considered blasphemous toward the memory of the dead in Roman thought. He then positioned his new basilica in honor of Peter at such an odd angle that he had to fill in a whole side of the hill with support walls. The only possible reason for this violation of sacred Roman traditions was to center his altar over the revered tomb of the apostle.

Another wonderful tradition about Peter's presence in Rome also grew up in later tradition. St. Ambrose first told it in one of his sermons. When the persecution of Nero broke out, the Christian community urged Peter to flee Rome and save himself so that they would not lose their leader. Peter vacillated, but finally gave in and was escaping by night down the Appian Way toward the south when he met Jesus coming up the road toward Rome, carrying his cross. Peter, shocked, stopped and asked, *"Quo Vadis, Domine?"* (Where are you going, Lord?). Jesus answered that he was going to Rome to be crucified a second time. Peter realized that Jesus was going to take his place. Ashamed, he turned back, was arrested, and ordered to be crucified. Guilt-ridden over his failure once again to acknowledge his Lord, he insisted that they turn the cross upside down because he was not worthy to die the way Jesus had been crucified. There may be no historical basis for this story, but it is a wonderful parable of Peter and his deep devotion to Jesus, even if he was somewhat lacking in courage!

Chapter 30

PAUL IS EXECUTED AND BURIED IN ROME

In the summer of 64 AD a great fire broke out in Rome that raged for nine days and devastated nearly the entire city, so that only four of its fourteen neighborhoods were spared. The Roman historian Tacitus lived through the fire as a boy and recorded later how it spread so rapidly that people had nowhere to find safe escape. As they fled in every direction, the flames seemed to jump over them and block the streets ahead. Thousands ended up standing in the countryside and on roads outside the city with nowhere to go. The emperor Nero had responded to the tragedy by ordering food for the people to be sent in immediately from the port of Ostia, and by opening up the army barracks and his palace grounds for refugees, but even these were soon consumed by flames. Another Roman writer, Suetonius, reported that rumors began to spread through the crowds of refugees that Nero himself had set the fire so that he could rebuild the center of the city in a more elegant fashion, and that he played a lyre and sang the lyrics from Homer's *Iliad* on the sack of Troy by the Greeks while he watched the flames from his balcony. There is no proof that Nero had any hand in the fire, but Suetonius was convinced that he did. He even reports eyewitnesses who saw Nero's servants setting the fires. In any case, Nero needed a scapegoat on whom to blame the fire quickly. Tacitus explained that he blamed the fire on the Christians who lived near the area of the Circus Maximus where the fire had begun, and whose religious beliefs were already considered suspect by many Romans (remember Claudius's decree against the followers of "Chrestus" in 49 AD in the chapters, "Paul's Ministry in Corinth" and "Paul Writes to Rome," above). Nero made an overwhelming public sport of the executions, having Christians torn apart by lions, or sewn into animal skins and fed to other beasts, or crucified and set on fire as torches to light the night sky. Many Christians died at this time, and it would not be unlikely that Paul and Peter may have been among the victims, although no ancient source claims that they died in the fire or the immediate Christian persecution that followed. We saw in the last chapter that Eusebius placed their deaths three years later in 67 AD.

What is certain is that the only first-century report about the deaths of the apostles is in the Letter of Pope Clement to the Corinthians, which was mentioned in the previous chapter about Paul's ministry in Spain. Because it was certainly written before the end of the first century, it was thus written within living memory of the events. Clement says that the two apostles were martyred under Nero, Paul by beheading and Peter by crucifixion, and that both were buried in Rome. Since Nero committed suicide in 68 AD, when his own Praetorian Guard turned against him, we can assume that Paul died somewhere between 64 and 67 AD. Because he was a Roman citizen, he could not be crucified but was entitled to execution by beheading. According to a third-century tradition, he was taken for execution to a place called *ad aquas salvius* ("The Salvian Spring"). This place is today called *Tre Fontane* ("The Three Fountains"), from the further legend that when his head fell from his body, it bounced three times on the ground, and at each bounce, a spring erupted from the earth. A shrine was eventually built over the site. But the disciples brought his body a little way down the Ostian Way to a cemetery nearer to the city. To this day, the Church of St. Paul Outside the Walls in Rome commemorates that place where the Christians buried his body.

There is thus no evidence of exactly when or by what means he actually died, but the second-century work, *The Acts of Paul and Thecla*, imaginatively describes his final confrontation with Nero in which the emperor accuses him of raising soldiers in his Empire to overthrow his rule, and Paul responds that he is not just raising soldiers in the Empire but over the whole world. The enraged Nero orders him to be beheaded. After his death, Paul appears to Nero in a vision in the middle of his entire court and predicts his horrible death to come. In the third century, a writer composed the *Letters of Seneca*, which consisted of a number of letters exchanged between Paul and Seneca, the Stoic philosopher who was the teacher of Nero. In them, Paul presents his Gospel message in a philosophical manner, and Seneca comes to believe in Paul's preaching and laments that Paul will be executed by Nero. A century later, St.

John Chrysostom repeats a story that tells how Paul converted a concubine of Nero, and as a result the emperor condemned him to death in a fit of jealousy. These are just a few of the many legends that grew up around Paul's life and death. He was so towering in his influence in the early church that wherever there seemed to be a gap or some uncertainty in his life story, it gave rise to a legend attributing acts of great faith to him.

Epilogue

LATER TRADITIONS ABOUT PAUL

A very early painting of Peter has been found in the Christian house-church excavated at Dura Europus in the eastern Empire on the Euphrates that dates from 232 AD. In the scene of Christ walking on the water, a bearded, curly-haired Peter is clearly sinking in the waves. Slightly later, about 280, there is a rough picture of a bald-headed man who is old and wrinkled, with a pointed beard, in the mausoleum of the Valerii, a part of the old cemetery beneath the Vatican. Inscribed next to the picture are the words, "Peter, pray to Jesus Christ for the holy Christians buried near your body." In the fourth century, many fine Christian sarcophagi found in Rome show scenes from the New Testament with Peter in them.

Roman legend has always maintained that Peter and Paul were imprisoned in the Mamertine Prison together before their execution, but there is no early confirmation of such a meeting. See the chapter "Paul Meets Peter in Rome (or Did He?)" above. The one reliable tradition that they did spend time together, even if only in death, comes two centuries later during the persecution of Decius, about 250, when the bodies of Paul and Peter were removed from their tombs on the Ostian Way and the Vatican Hill respectively, and brought to a hiding place, *ad catacumbas*. This refers to the famous catacombs of St. Sebastian on the Appian Way. A *cumba* is a ground depression, and near this natural hollow the tufa soil was very easy to dig, and so the Christians had built an extended underground cemetery in corridors through the soft rock. One ample room was added about this time for large gatherings, and on the surviving plaster walls were found many graffiti inscriptions like the following: "Peter and Paul, pray for Victor!" "Peter and Paul, do not forget Antonius Bassus." "Tomius Coelius made a feast in honor of Peter and Paul." It certainly indicates that the temporary resting places of the two apostles must have been together and very near to the inscriptions. Presumably their bodies were returned to their original graves when the danger passed.

95